10 Things
Pope Benedict XVI
Wants You to Know

st
ey

de-

10 Things
Pope Benedict XVI
Wants You to Know

John L. Allen, Jr.

Liguori
ONE LIGUORI DRIVE
LIGUORI MO 63057-9999

Imprimi Potest:
Thomas D. Picton, C.Ss.R.
Provincial, Denver Province
The Redemptorists

ISBN 978-0-7648-1672-7
Copyright 2007, Liguori Publications
Printed in the United States of America
07 08 09 10 11 5 4 3 2 1

Excerpts from *Deus Caritas Est; Sacramentum Caritatis;* homilies, speeches, and letters of Pope Benedict XVI used with permission of Libreria Editrice Vaticana, Città del Vaticano - cap 00120; Via della Tipografia; Italy. All rights reserved.

Excerpts from *Jesus of Nazareth* used with permission from RCS MediaGroup S.p.A., Via San Marco 21; 20121 Milan, Italy. All rights reserved.

Excerpts from the *Ratzinger Report* (*Rapporto Sulla Fede*, 1985) and Homily for World Youth Day, 2005, used with permission of Edizioni San Paulo, Piazza Soncino, 5-20092; Cinisello Balsamo (Milano), Italy. All rights reserved.

Liguori Publications, a nonprofit corporation, is an apos-tolate of the Redemptorists. To learn more about the Redemptorists, visit Redemptorists.com.

To order, call 1-800-325-9521
www.liguori.org

Introduction

THOUGH POPE BENEDICT XVI is one of the most accomplished Roman Catholic theologians of his era, the aim of his pontificate is not the construction of a new "grand theory" for Catholic theology. Neither is his goal to remake the Catholic Church according to the personal tastes and inclinations of Joseph Ratzinger. Instead, Benedict's top priority is to reintroduce the fundamentals of the Christian gospel and of Catholic tradition to the modern world, striving to illustrate their coherence with the deepest truths of human existence. Benedict doesn't want to put a new gloss on the basic teachings of Catholicism; rather, he wants to lead contemporary men and women to see those teachings with fresh eyes, setting aside the prejudices and assumptions accumulated over the course of the centuries.

That's the spirit of this overview of the ten things Benedict XVI wants you to know.

You won't find a lot of complicated theological concepts or breathtaking new ideas, for Benedict isn't interested in pushing the envelope of theological discussion. What's creative about him is, rather, the fresh way he explains core Christian teachings. Benedict is a pope of "the basics," which he presents in an intelligent, provocative fashion, striving to make clear that Christianity is not merely a set of rules but a resounding "yes" to the dignity of the human person and the embrace of a loving God.

One other introductory note. The English Jesuit George Tyrell once accused nineteenth-century biblical scholars who had gone in quest of the "historical Jesus" of peering into a deep well and seeing only themselves in the reflection. The phrase has become a metaphor for writers who couch their work as an analysis of some other figure but who are really projecting their own ideas and visions. Aware of that danger, I don't intend this short overview to be John Allen's version of Pope Benedict. As much as possible, we'll stick to Benedict's own thought and words, so that it is the real pontiff who speaks to us.

1

God Is Love

STRIP EVERYTHING else away, and the core of the Christian message is that God is love. The ultimate reality in the universe, the one which created it and sustains it, is love. In faith, we call that personal love God. Since that's the point upon which everything else in Christianity pivots, it's no surprise that Pope Benedict chose to title his very first encyclical, the most important form of papal teaching, *Deus Caritas Est*—precisely, "God Is Love."

The heart of the encyclical's argument is that *eros,* or human sexual love, is a beautiful reflection of God's passionate love for humanity. Yet *eros,* he says, is not an end in itself. Rather, it calls us out of ourselves, toward something even higher. *Eros* must be transformed through "a path of ascent, renunciation, purification and healing" into *agape*, meaning the complete gift of oneself for another. *Agape,* in turn, flows into service of one's neighbor, especially the poor and vulnerable, which is the basis for all Catholic charitable work. In order for this purification to happen, we have to exercise our reason about the right way to put our love into action. Thus, Benedict says, a final element of the Christian concept of love is *logos*—referring not only to "words" in the sense of human thought, but also to the Word, the Son of God, made flesh in Jesus Christ.

Against any abstract or purely philosophical concept of God, *Deus Caritas Est* reminds us that the Christian God is not just a force or a concept, but a lover.

"God is the absolute and ultimate source of all being; but this universal principle of creation—the *Logos*, primordial reason—is at the same time a lover with all the passion of a true love," Benedict writes. The late Italian Vatican writer Orazio Petrosillo said that with *Deus Caritas Est*, Joseph Ratzinger, once known as *Il Grande Inquisitore*, or "the Grand Inquisitor," revealed himself as *Il Grande Innamorato*, or "the Great Lover."

Benedict is well aware that critics over the centuries, such as Friedrich Nietzsche, have complained that Christianity "ruined" *eros* by making human beings ashamed of their sexuality, by treating sex as something to be controlled and feared. Instead, Benedict argues, Christianity liberates *eros* by pointing the way toward its true fulfillment.

The pope chose to write on this theme, at this time, in part out of concern for all the violence and hatred in today's world justified in the name of a loving God. Too often, Benedict believes, people mistake passion for love, as if all we need is the heart, not the head. In reality, the pope insists, feeling is just the beginning of love, not the end. At bottom, love is the recognition that we are the sons and daughters of God's love for all humanity, which calls us to love of our neighbor—all our neighbors, everywhere in the world.

Benedict's understanding of love is closer to that of Dostoevsky in *The Brothers Karamazov*, who wrote, "Love in action is a harsh and dreadful thing compared to love in dreams." Real love comes at a price. That's the kind of love we see in Jesus, and that's the kind of love that Benedict describes in *Deus Caritas Est*.

2

Jesus Is Lord

BENEDICT XVI has always been a prodigious
writer, and in May 2007 he released the first
book of his papacy: *Jesus of Nazareth*, a 400-
page work that's projected as the first vol-
ume of a longer study. In essence, Benedict
wants to assure his readers that the gospels
are reliable witnesses to Jesus. They teach us
that the Jesus of history and the Christ of
faith are one and the same figure: the Living Son of God, made flesh. Placing Christ
at the center is Benedict's *modus operandi,*
and proper "Christology," meaning teaching
about Christ, is the dominant doctrinal concern of his papacy.

Benedict wrote the book in part because
during the last century, a number of popular reinterpretations of Jesus were floated by
Bible scholars and theologians, usually in an
effort to make Jesus more "relevant." But the

pope believes that starting with desired social outcomes and then drawing conclusions
about Jesus puts the cart before the horse.
There can be no humane social order or last-
ing moral progress, he says, apart from a
right relationship with God, and it is Jesus
Christ who reveals God's face to us. If we really want to promote justice and tolerance,
Benedict says, we have to start with Christ.
Preaching Christ is not a distraction, he believes, from building a better world—it *is*
building a better world.

Over the course of the book, Benedict cri-
tiques a number of popular modern images
of Jesus: Jesus as a preacher of liberal moral-
ity, Jesus as a social revolutionary, Jesus as an
inspired prophet or sage on the level of other
founders of religious movements. The pope
is well aware that these interpretations usually arise from noble motives, which he also
shares—to affirm the primacy of human beings over the law, to combat poverty and
injustice, and to express tolerance for other
religions. But out of impatience to achieve
desired social outcomes, Benedict argues,
revisionist images of Jesus subvert the only

basis for real humanism, which is belief in
God, and in an objective truth that comes
from God and stands above the human will
to power.

Reflecting on Christ's temptations in the
desert, Benedict makes this argument:

*Whenever God is considered a secondary con-
cern, which can temporarily or stably be set
aside in the name of more important things,
then it is precisely those things presumed to
be more important which fail. It's not just the
negative result of Marxism which makes the
point. The aid given by the West to developing
countries, based purely on technical-materi
al principles, which has not only left God to
the side but has also distanced people from
God with the pride of its presumed superior
wisdom, has made the Third World into the
"Third World" in the modern sense....Believ-
ing it could transform stones into bread, it has
instead given stones in place of bread. What's
at stake is the primacy of God. It's a matter of
recognizing God as a reality, a reality without
which nothing else can be good. History cannot be governed with merely material struc-*

tures, prescinding from God. If the heart of the human person isn't good, then nothing else can be good. And goodness of heart can come only from He who is Himself goodness, who is the Good.

Reminding the world that, in Jesus of Nazareth, we see the definitive revelation of the meaning and ultimate destiny of human life, is a cornerstone of Benedict's papacy.

3

Truth and Freedom Are Two Sides of the Same Coin

IF ONE WERE LOOKING for a single word to sum up Benedict XVI's message to the men and women of his time, it might well be "truth." His motto as a bishop is *Cooperatores veritatis:* "coworkers of the truth." The day before the conclave opened that elected him to the papacy in April 2005, then–Joseph Cardinal Ratzinger memorably defined the chief challenge facing the Catholic Church as a "dictatorship of relativism." By that, he meant the way in which denial of objective truth—of truths independent of time and culture, binding everywhere and for everyone—has become conventional wisdom.

It's worth quoting the heart of that homily:

How many winds of doctrine have we known in these recent decades, how many ideological currents, how many modes of thought...The small ship of thought of many Christians has often been agitated by these waves—tossed from one extreme to the other; from Marxism to liberalism, from collectivism to radical individualism; from atheism to a vague religious mysticism; from agnosticism to syncretism and so on....To have a clear faith, according to the Creed of the Church, is often styled as fundamentalism. Meanwhile relativism, meaning allowing oneself to be carried away "here and there by any wind of doctrine," appears as the only attitude suited to modern times. What's being constructed is a dictatorship of relativism, which recognizes nothing as definitive, and that regards one's self and one's own desires as the final measure.

Benedict realizes that many people unconsciously endorse this "dictatorship of relativism" because they want to be free, meaning that they don't want to live on the basis of someone else's truths. But Benedict believes that such a desire reflects a flawed understanding of what freedom entails. Freedom, he believes, is not the absence of restraint on our behavior, but rather the capacity to become the kind of person God calls us to be. That doesn't mean doing whatever we want; it means doing what we should.

Put it this way: An alcoholic might imagine himself "free" as long as he's able to drink as much as he likes, but we know he won't really be "free" until he breaks the chains of his addiction. It's the same with all of us, Benedict believes. Real freedom does not mean freedom to exploit the poor, to hate one's neighbor, or to sacrifice unborn life; it means the freedom to realize our highest potential as sons and daughters of God. God wants us to be free, but this freedom has content—it means ordering our lives in accord with God's design. Truth and freedom are thus not opposed, but interdependent. Truth, for Benedict XVI, is the doorway through which one must walk in order to be "free" in the fullest sense of the word.

4

Faith and Reason Need One Another

ON SEPTEMBER 12, 2006, Benedict XVI gave a lecture at the University of Regensburg in Germany, where he once taught theology. That lecture became a "shot heard 'round the world" because of controversies surrounding a quotation from a dialogue between a fourteenth-century Byzantine emperor and a Persian scholar, in which the emperor said negative things about Muhammad, the founder of Islam. The ensuing firestorm was unfortunate, in part because few people read the whole lecture—which was not about Islam at all, but the relationship between reason and faith. The title, in fact, was "Faith, Reason and the University."

Benedict XVI summed up the testimony of the Bible and the early Christian church in the following fashion: God is *Logos,* creative reason itself. Thus, "not to act in accordance with reason is contrary to God's nature." Christianity presupposes the rationality of God, and on the basis of that conviction, Christianity itself must be reasonable. Shutting down the exercise of human reason, turning Christianity into a form of religious fundamentalism, would be inconsistent with the rational character of God himself.

More broadly, Benedict said, faith and reason desperately need one another.

In the first place, Benedict argues, faith and reason belong together because reason presumes faith. How do scientists know that there's an underlying logic to the universe? Why do they assume that nature will work tomorrow the way it did yesterday? Why do they believe the human mind is capable of penetrating nature's secrets? In the end, they take all this on faith—a stance grounded in the Judeo-Christian tradition, whether today's scientists acknowledge it or not.

On another level, much dysfunction in contemporary culture, Benedict believes, can be explained by attempts to separate reason and faith. Reason without faith, he believes, becomes skepticism, cynicism, and ultimately nihilism, leading to despair. Faith without reason, on the other hand, becomes fundamentalism, extremism, and sometimes violence. We see this today in radical currents within Islam, which justify terrorism and hatred in the name of God. Benedict is well aware, however, that in a different key, the same temptation to irrationality courses through every religion, which makes it all the more important that faith and reason remain on speaking terms.

5

The Eucharist Is the Heart of the Christian Life

WHEN POPE BENEDICT XVI went to Cologne, Germany, for World Youth Day in August 2005, many Germans expected the pope to take them to task on a variety of fronts—from declining Mass attendance and internal dissent within the Church, to a general unwillingness to grant religion a role in public life. Instead, Benedict offered a message that was at the same time more gentle and yet more radical. In his concluding homily, he chose to meditate on the Eucharist, Christ's gift of himself under the forms of bread and wine at Mass.

The pope offered a memorable metaphor to describe its impact. He told the one million young people who had gathered to hear him:

To use an image well known to us today, [consecrating the Eucharist] is like inducing nuclear fission in the very heart of being— the victory of love over hatred, the victory of love over death, Only this intimate explosion of good conquering evil can then trigger off the series of transformations that little by little will change the world. All other changes remain superficial and cannot save. For this reason we speak of redemption: what had to happen at the most intimate level has indeed happened, and we can enter into its dynamic. Jesus can distribute his Body, because he truly gives himself.

That imagery came from Joseph Ratzinger's lifetime of prayer and devotion centered on the Eucharist.

In March 2007, Benedict XVI released a document called an "apostolic exhortation," officially drawing conclusions from the Synod of Bishops on the Eucharist that took place in the Vatican in October 2005. It's titled *Sacramentum Caritatis* (Sacrament of Charity) and it offers Benedict's most developed reflections on the Eucharist.

The Church's faith is essentially a Eucharistic faith, and it is especially nourished at the table of the Eucharist....For this reason, the Sacrament of the Altar is always at the heart of the Church's life...The more lively the eucharistic faith of the People of God, the deeper is its sharing in ecclesial life in steadfast commitment to the mission entrusted by Christ to his disciples.

That last line is important, because as Benedict goes on to argue in *Sacramentum Caritatis,* the faith expressed in the Eucharist comes with a mission. On a personal level, it impels us to live our lives in accordance with what we profess during the Mass; we must become, as Saint Augustine once famously suggested, what we consume, meaning to model ourselves on Christ. On a social level, it means efforts to build a world in which the self-giving love of Christ, which is made new each time the Eucharist is celebrated, is the cornerstone upon which society is constructed, as opposed to ideology, profit, or the blind will to power.

Taken seriously, Benedict argues, the Eucharist can change the world—indeed, it's the only thing that can.

6

Christianity Is a Positive Message

ONE OF THE MOST striking aspects of Benedict XVI's papacy has been how determined he is to phrase his message in a positive key. To take one example, when the Holy Father visited Spain in July 2006, many expected a dramatic showdown with the Socialist government of Prime Minister José Luis Rodríguez Zapatero, whose left-wing government has done battle with the Church on a variety of fronts: gay marriage, abortion, divorce, euthanasia, and public funding for Catholic schools. Many Catholics expected fire and brimstone from the pope. Instead, he was doggedly positive, concentrating on the Christian fundamentals, never directly engaging any of the issues that have divided Church and state.

Later, some German TV reporters asked Benedict what had happened. It's worth listening to his reply in full:

Christianity, Catholicism, isn't a collection of prohibitions: it's a positive option. It's very important that we look at it again because this idea has almost completely disappeared today. We've heard so much about what is not allowed that now it's time to say: we have a positive idea to offer, that man and woman are made for each other, that the scale of sexuality, eros, agape, indicates the level of love and it's in this way that marriage develops, first of all, as a joyful and blessing-filled encounter between a man and a woman, and then the family, that guarantees continuity among generations and through which generations are reconciled to each other and even cultures can meet. So, firstly it's important to stress what we want. Secondly, we can also see why we don't want something. I believe we need to see and reflect on the fact that it's not a Catholic invention that man and woman are made for each other, so that humanity can go on living: all cultures know this. As far as abortion is concerned, it's part of the fifth, not the sixth, commandment: 'Thou shalt not kill!' We have to presume this is obvious and always stress that the human person begins in the mother's womb and remains a human person until his or her last breath. The human person must always be respected as a human person. But all this is clearer if you say it first in a positive way.

Benedict's desire is to lead contemporary Catholics back to the fundamentals of our faith, to remind us of that deep "yes" that lies beneath our specific "no's" on hot-button cultural debates.

During his May 2007 trip to Brazil, Benedict XVI put the same point a different way when he said:

The Church does not engage in proselytism. Instead, she grows by "attraction": just as Christ "draws all to himself" by the power of his love, culminating in the sacrifice of the Cross, so the Church fulfils her mission to the extent that, in union with Christ, she accomplishes every one of her works in spiritual and practical imitation of the love of her Lord.

In other words, the pope wants Christians to let the "good news" of their faith shine through their own lives, so that its inner beauty can again become clear in a world accustomed to thinking of Christianity as little more than a fussy legal system. That doesn't make the law less important or valid, but Benedict realizes that one doesn't stir hearts with law, but with love.

7

The Church Forms Consciences but Stays Out of Politics

OVER THE COURSE of his career as a theologian and a Church official, Benedict XVI has resisted any attempt to turn Christianity into a political party. That doesn't mean, however, that faith lacks consequences for politics. Benedict wrote in his first encyclical, *Deus Caritas Est,* that "Justice is both the aim and the intrinsic criterion of all politics." According to the moral vision of Benedict XVI, a Christian must work toward a just social order, which among other things implies a special concern for the poor.

In an address to the bishops of Latin America and the Caribbean on May 13, 2007, Benedict endorsed what exponents of liberation theology have called the "preferential option for the poor," saying it is "implicit in the Christological faith in the God who became poor for us." And he has not shrunk from drawing the consequences of this option.

Benedict has repeatedly spoken out in defense of the poor, often in language with very concrete political implications. For example, in December 2006, he wrote to German Chancellor Angela Merkel, at the time the president of the G8 group of nations, demanding "the rapid, total and unconditional cancellation" of the external debt of poor countries. The pope described debt relief as a "grave and unconditional moral responsibility, founded on the unity of the human race, and on the common dignity and shared destiny of rich and poor alike."

Benedict has shown a special pastoral concern for the struggles of Africa. In June 2005 he announced his intention to call a synod of bishops from Africa to discuss the crises facing the continent. In November 2006, when a new bond measure was launched by the World Bank to raise four billion dollars over ten years for the immunization of children in impoverished nations against preventable diseases, the very first bond was purchased by Pope Benedict XVI.

For Benedict XVI, fidelity to Church teaching and Tradition is not opposed to social concern; to conceive of things that way, he believes, would be to pit faith against works, a position Roman Catholicism rejected during the Protestant Reformation more than five hundred years ago.

At the same time, Benedict is clear that the role of the Church is to hold up moral values, not to provide a specific political blueprint for translating those values into political choices. "If the church were to start transforming herself into a directly political subject, she would do less, not more, for the poor and for justice," the pope said during his trip to Brazil, "because she would lose her independence and her moral authority, identifying herself with a single political path and with debatable partisan positions."

"The church is the advocate of justice and of the poor, precisely because she does not identify with politicians nor with partisan interests," Benedict continued. "Only by remaining independent can she teach the great criteria and inalienable values, guide consciences and offer a life choice that goes beyond the political sphere."

8

The Importance of Catholic Identity

IN A MARCH 20, 2007, address to Italian businesspeople, Tarcisio Cardinal Bertone, the Vatican's Secretary of State and a long-time intimate of Pope Benedict XVI, said that the "overall goal" of Benedict's papacy is to defend authentic Christian identity in a world marked by religious relativism.

This thrust toward a stronger sense of identity forms one of the megatrends in contemporary Catholicism. In every area of the life of the Church—from liturgy to religious orders, from Catholic schools and hospitals to seminary instruction—the question of the day is, "How do we know it's Catholic, and how do we make sure it stays Catholic?"

A consummate student of Western culture, Benedict knows that since the Peace of

Westphalia in 1648, religion has suffered a progressive exile from public life, especially in Europe. In the West today, religion is often seen as a purely private matter, and religious people feel pressure to either downplay or abandon those aspects of their faith that don't "fit" with the values of enlightened modern culture. Over time, Benedict worries, in too many areas the Catholic Church has gradually assimilated to this ethos, absorbing its worldview like secondhand smoke. The result is that some Catholics, and some Catholic institutions, are shaped more by the values of secular modernity than the tradition of the Church.

The time has come, Benedict believes, to recover a strong sense of what makes Catholics different. His decisions in July 2007 to broaden permission for use of the pre–Vatican II Mass, and to reassert that the Catholic Church alone is the true church willed by Christ, both express this conviction.

Benedict XVI comes out of the *Communio* school in Catholic theology, associated above all with the great twentieth-century Swiss theologian Hans Urs von Balthasar. Its key figures accent the need for the Church to speak its own language, premised on the conviction that Christianity is itself a culture, often at odds with the prevailing worldview of modernity. Restoring a sense of Catholic distinctiveness—a Catholic version of what sociologists call the "politics of identity"—has in some ways been Joseph Ratzinger's life's work.

In that light, Pope Benedict is less immediately concerned with numbers, such as Mass attendance or turnout at papal events, than with fostering a deep sense of Catholic distinctiveness, however few those who embrace such a spirit may be.

As early as *The Ratzinger Report* in 1984, he put things this way: "Today more than ever, the Christian must be aware that he belongs to a minority and that he is in opposition to everything that appears good, obvious, and logical to the 'spirit of the world,' as the New Testament calls it. Among the most urgent tasks facing Christians is that of regaining the capacity of non-conformism, i.e., the capacity to oppose many developments of the surrounding culture."

That doesn't mean, of course, that Benedict wants Christians to cut themselves off from the world, retreating into a Catholic ghetto. Rather, he wants them to be *in* the world but not *of* it—to find, as he once memorably put it, "that none-too-easy balance between a proper incarnation in history, and the indispensable tension toward eternity."

9
Christ and the Church Are Inseparable

IN MARCH 2006, Benedict XVI announced that he would devote his catechesis during his regular Wednesday General Audiences that spring to the "profound, inseparable, and mysterious continuity" between Jesus and the Church. Any attempt to say "yes" to Jesus but "no" to the Church, Benedict insisted, ultimately falls apart, because Jesus' message was intended precisely "to gather and to save" a people, which is the Church.

The Wednesday catechesis is the most important regular opportunity a pope has to get his message across, and for a teaching pope such as Benedict XVI, the choice of theme is revealing in terms of his priorities. Benedict is well aware that for many contemporary men and women, Jesus of Nazareth remains a fascinating figure, but they often struggle with aspects of institutional religion. The natural temptation, therefore, is to opt for Jesus without the "intermediary" of the Church.

In the end, however, one cannot truly love Jesus or follow his teachings, Benedict insists, without taking one's place in the family of faith that Jesus called into being. Being part of that family comes with no guarantees of perfect contentment; like any family, the Church has its ups and downs, its moments of disappointment and heartache. If that's true of a human family, how much more it is of a global Church of more than one billion people, carrying the weight of two thousand years of history! But just as one does not walk away from a family when things get rough, similarly a disciple of Jesus does not walk away from his or her Church.

Describing as "baseless" any "individualistic interpretation of the proclamation about the Kingdom made by Christ," Benedict said that the "obvious intent" of Jesus "was to unite the community of the covenant" into "the Twelve," symbolized and led by the twelve apostles.

"By their very existence, the Twelve—called from diverse origins—become an appeal to all Israel to convert, and to allow itself to be gathered into the new covenant, a full and perfect fulfillment of the old one," the pope said. "By entrusting the Twelve with the task of celebrating his memory in the Supper before his Passion, Jesus showed that he wanted to transfer to the whole community, in the person of his leaders, the mandate of being a sign and instrument of eschatological oneness throughout history, started in him. In this light, one understands how the Resurrected One conferred upon them, with the effusion of the Spirit, the power to forgive sins (cfr John 20:23). The Twelve Apostles are thus the most evident sign of the will of Jesus regarding the existence and mission of His Church, the guarantee that between Christ and the Church, there is no contraposition."

In response to the cry of "Yes to Jesus, No to the Church," Benedict XVI responds, "Yes to Jesus *means* Yes to the Church."

10

The Virtue of Patience

SAINT AUGUSTINE once wrote that "the deeds of the Word are, for us, words too." He meant that we learn as much from what Jesus did as from what Jesus said.

In a similar vein, popes teach the world through their actions, their personalities, and their "styles," in addition to their explicit speech. For example, perhaps one of the most eloquent moments of John Paul II's papacy came near the end on Easter Sunday 2005, when despite his obvious agony, he spent twelve long minutes at the window of his apartment, struggling to speak to the faithful gathered below in Saint Peter's Square and to the millions watching around the world. The way John Paul poured himself out in service that day spoke volumes about his self-sacrifice, even though he never managed to utter a single word.

Probably without being conscious of it, Pope Benedict XVI is teaching the world something through his own behavior. He is exceedingly humble and gentle, which stands in stark contrast to the bluster and braggadocio often associated with global titans in the worlds of politics, finance, and culture. He is living proof that one does not have to be an exhibitionist to lead and to inspire.

Perhaps more important, he's teaching a microwave world that expects instant results to slow down a bit, to catch its breath, and to look before it leaps. Upon Benedict's election, there were fevered expectations of swift and dramatic action in many quarters. Some expected a root-and-branch reform of the Roman Curia, the Catholic Church's central organ of government. Others anticipated a sweeping crackdown on dissident theologians and liberal activists within the Church. To this day, many pundits and commentators are still waiting for the "real" Benedict to emerge from beneath his patient, gentle façade; what they don't seem to appreciate is that what they regard as a façade is, in fact, the real pope.

Benedict is a man of deep faith, which means he realizes that, ultimately, the vicissitudes of the Church and of the world are in God's hands, not his. There's a serenity about him, a lack of what the Germans call *angst*, rooted in his belief that the final act of the story in which all of us are involved has already been written, and it ends well. Thus he does not feel the need to lurch from one initiative to the next or to resolve all the Church's problems in a single bound. He understands better than most the complexities of those problems, both intellectually and pastorally, and he also grasps the importance of thinking carefully before taking steps that may have unforeseen consequences.

In an impatient world, Benedict XVI is a very patient man. To paraphrase Saint Augustine, occasionally his very *lack* of deeds is an important "word" for the harried women and men of his time.

About the Author

JOHN L. ALLEN, JR., is the senior correspondent for the *National Catholic Reporter* and senior Vatican analyst for CNN. He's also the author of *The Rise of Benedict XVI* (Doubleday, 2005) and the forthcoming book, *Mega-Trends in Catholicism: Ten Forces Turning the Catholic Church Upside Down* (Doubleday, 2008).